Turning Points in History

THE BOMBING OF HIROSHIMA AND NAGASAKI

Nick Rebman

WWW.APEXEDITIONS.COM

Copyright © 2025 by Apex Editions, Mendota Heights, MN 55120. All rights reserved. No part of this book may be reproduced or utilized in any form or by any means without written permission from the publisher.

Apex is distributed by North Star Editions:
sales@northstareditions.com | 888-417-0195

Produced for Apex by Red Line Editorial.

Photographs ©: United States Army Air Forces/Library of Congress, cover, 1; Hulton Archive/Archive Photos/Getty Images, 4–5; Roger Viollet/Getty Images, 6–7; US Signal Corps/AP Images, 8–9, 58; National Park Service, 10–11; National Archives, 12–13, 38–39; Bettmann/Getty Images, 14–15, 52–53, 54–55; AP Images, 16–17, 36–37; Hulton-Deutsch Collection/Corbis Historical/Getty Images, 18–19; Corbis Historical/Getty Images, 20–21, 22–23, 29, 30–31, 48–49; Shutterstock Images, 24–25, 50–51; Library of Congress, 26–27; Joe Rosenthal/AP Images, 32–33; Universal History Archive/Universal Images Group/Getty Images, 34–35; Galerie Bilderwelt/Hulton Archive/Getty Images, 40–41; FPG/Hulton Archive/Archive Photos/Getty Images, 42–43; Afro American Newspapers/Gado/Archive Photos/Getty Images, 44–45; Jemal Countess/WireImage/Getty Images, 47; Takuya Yoshino/Yomiuri Shimbun/AP Images, 56–57

Library of Congress Control Number: 2024942356

ISBN
979-8-89250-461-4 (hardcover)
979-8-89250-477-5 (paperback)
979-8-89250-507-9 (ebook pdf)
979-8-89250-493-5 (hosted ebook)

Printed in the United States of America
Mankato, MN
012025

NOTE TO PARENTS AND EDUCATORS

Apex books are designed to build literacy skills in striving readers. Exciting, high-interest content attracts and holds readers' attention. The text is carefully leveled to allow students to achieve success quickly.

TABLE OF CONTENTS

Chapter 1
DEATH AND DESTRUCTION 4

Chapter 2
WAR IN THE PACIFIC 10

Chapter 3
THE MANHATTAN PROJECT 20

Story Spotlight
J. ROBERT OPPENHEIMER 28

Chapter 4
HIROSHIMA 30

Chapter 5
NAGASAKI 39

Story Spotlight
DOUBLE SURVIVOR 46

Chapter 6
LEGACY 48

TIMELINE • 59
COMPREHENSION QUESTIONS • 60
GLOSSARY • 62
TO LEARN MORE • 63
ABOUT THE AUTHOR • 63
INDEX • 64

Chapter 1

DEATH AND DESTRUCTION

On August 6, 1945, a US plane flew high over Hiroshima, Japan. World War II (1939–1945) had been going on for nearly six years. The plane dropped a powerful new type of bomb. This bomb exploded over the city. There was a blinding flash of light.

The bombing of Hiroshima created a mushroom cloud that was taller than Earth's highest mountains.

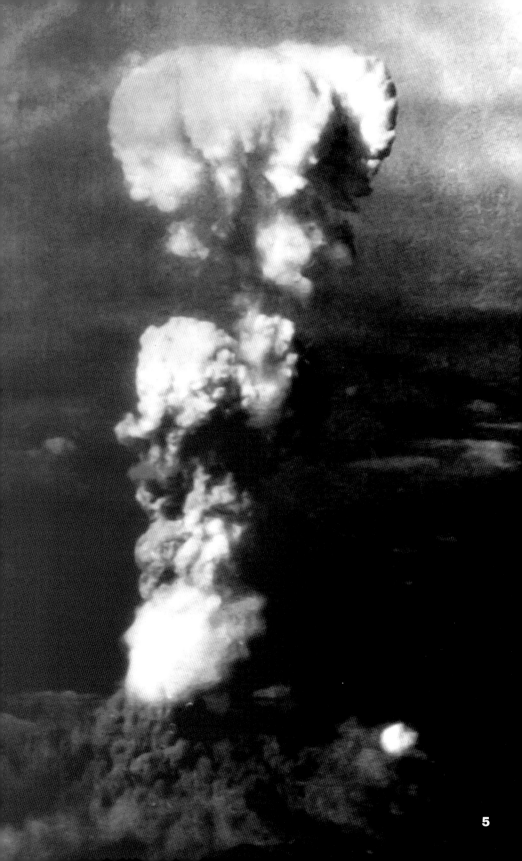

The blast created a huge fireball. An enormous mushroom cloud rose several miles high. Windows shattered. Buildings crumbled. Birds exploded into flames. Temperatures on the ground reached thousands of degrees.

At least 70,000 people died instantly. Many more were horribly hurt. Some people had burns all over their bodies. Some were cut by flying glass. Others were hit by flying rubble.

The bomb created fires that made a huge cloud of smoke. This cloud was even larger than the mushroom cloud.

The city of Hiroshima was almost completely destroyed by the bomb.

Survivors crawled out from the rubble. They tried to help one another. But there was little they could do. Fires burned all over the city. Many people could not escape. Thousands more died in the flames.

FIRESTORM

Most of Hiroshima's buildings were made of wood. As a result, flames spread quickly. Soon, many fires joined together. They created one huge fire. It caused a firestorm. That is when a fire's heat causes strong winds.

Chapter 2

WAR IN THE PACIFIC

On December 7, 1941, Japan attacked the United States. Japanese planes bombed Pearl Harbor. This harbor was in Hawai'i. The planes destroyed many US ships. More than 2,400 people were killed.

The attack on Pearl Harbor damaged 21 US ships. It also destroyed more than 180 aircraft.

The attack on Pearl Harbor caused the United States to enter World War II. The United States joined the Allies. This group of countries fought the Axis powers. That group included Japan. Some Allied battles with Japan took place at sea. Others happened on land.

ISLAND-HOPPING

Japan controlled many Pacific islands. Some islands had heavy defenses. The Allies didn't attack those. Instead, they captured islands with light defenses. Then, the Allies blocked Japan's supply lines. Without supplies, other islands had to give up.

The Battle of Midway in 1942 was a major US victory in the Pacific.

Filipino and US forces freed the Philippines from Japan in 1945.

Japan had already conquered several countries in Asia. Japan took over Korea in 1905. In 1931, Japan invaded China. By 1942, Japan also controlled most of Southeast Asia. Japan's rule was brutal. Millions of people died.

Little by little, the Allies won. They regained the areas Japan had taken over. By June 1945, Japan only had its home islands.

WAR CRIMES

In several countries, Japanese soldiers killed huge groups of civilians. They beat prisoners and forced them to work. Soldiers assaulted many women, too. These acts are war crimes.

In 1945, the United States firebombed Japanese cities. US planes dropped many firebombs. The blasts did not cause major damage. But they created lots of fires. These fires spread quickly. They formed a firestorm.

Firebombing raids did not target soldiers or factories. Instead, the raids hit areas where civilians lived. Hundreds of thousands of people died. Millions more lost their homes.

A firebombing raid in Tokyo killed 100,000 people in one night.

Japan's leaders feared that the United States would force out Emperor Hirohito (above). That was one reason why they did not stop fighting.

Japan suffered heavy losses. But the country didn't give up. So, the Allies made new plans. Leaders talked about invading Japan. Planners thought the fighting would be very deadly. They studied recent battles. One was at Okinawa. Many soldiers died defending this island. Planners thought even more would fight to protect Japan's main islands.

A COUNTRY DIVIDED

The Allies told Japan to give up. Many people in Japan wanted the war to end. But Japan's military leaders decided to keep fighting. They hoped to win a big battle. That way, Japan might get a better peace deal.

Chapter 3

THE MANHATTAN PROJECT

Meanwhile, US scientists were working on a new type of weapon. Back in 1938, scientists had learned nuclear bombs could be built. US leaders worried that enemies would build one first. So, in 1942, President Franklin D. Roosevelt started a new program. It aimed to create a nuclear bomb.

Leo Szilard was a key scientist behind the development of nuclear bombs.

The project to make the bomb cost billions of dollars. It took three years.

The program was called the Manhattan Project. More than 130,000 people took part. They worked in labs across the United States. People did many different jobs. Most were told little about what they were doing. Very few knew they were making a bomb.

TOP SECRET

The Manhattan Project was top secret. Not even Vice President Harry S. Truman knew about it. However, President Roosevelt died on April 12, 1945. Truman became the new president. Military leaders soon told him about the project.

On July 16, 1945, a bomb was ready. Scientists tested it. They built a tower in the New Mexico desert. The bomb blew up at the top. It turned the tower into vapor. People saw the blast more than 200 miles (320 km) away. They said that it looked like a rising sun. The test was a success. The bomb could destroy a whole city.

SPLITTING ATOMS

Atoms are tiny pieces of matter. Scientists figured out how to split atoms. Splitting the atoms set off a chain reaction. That is what gave the bomb its power.

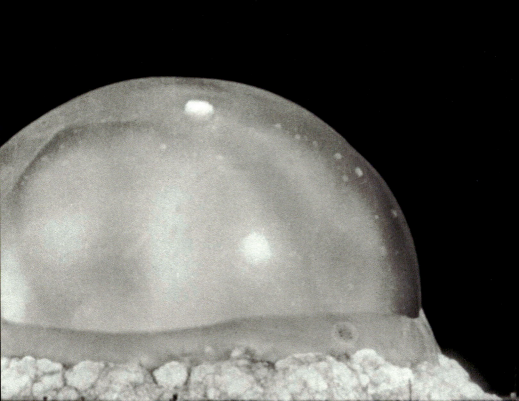

The first nuclear test was called the Trinity Test. The test harmed Indigenous people who lived nearby.

President Truman wanted to use the bomb against Japan. Some US leaders thought he should warn Japan first. He could drop a bomb somewhere without people. This would show the bomb's power. Then Japan might give up. However, Truman decided not to warn Japan. He wasn't sure the bomb would work. And if it did work, he wanted it to be a huge shock.

Harry S. Truman was the 33rd president of the United States.

Story Spotlight

J. ROBERT OPPENHEIMER

J. Robert Oppenheimer was a scientist who worked on the Manhattan Project. He led a lab in New Mexico. His team planned how to build the bomb. By 1944, they had two models ready. In July 1945, his team created the first nuclear bomb. He helped test it on July 16.

At first, Oppenheimer thought the bomb should be used against Japan. But after the war ended, he changed his views. He did not want more nuclear bombs to be built. He believed they were too dangerous.

J. Robert Oppenheimer felt guilty about the destruction he helped create.

Chapter 4
HIROSHIMA

US leaders began planning a nuclear attack. They wanted to win the war as soon as possible. They thought dropping a bomb could force Japan to give up. Then, US soldiers would not need to invade. Far fewer of them would die.

More than 16 million Americans served in World War II. More than 400,000 of them died in the war.

US leaders chose possible targets for the bomb. They created a list of five cities. Each city had factories. They made war supplies. US planners hoped to destroy the factories. That way, Japan would not be able to keep fighting.

DROPPING LEAFLETS

In the summer of 1945, US planes flew over Japanese cities. They dropped leaflets. The leaflets said attacks were likely. But they did not talk about nuclear bombs. Many people left cities. But many others were unable to leave.

Taking islands from Japan helped US forces focus on Japan's main islands. In March 1945, US soldiers took Iwo Jima.

People near the bomb died instantly. Some left only shadow-like shapes on buildings.

US leaders chose Hiroshima as the target. The city was a military center. On August 6, 1945, a US plane dropped a nuclear bomb on the city. The blast destroyed much of Hiroshima. It killed tens of thousands of people. Most were civilians.

DEATH TOLL

No one knows how many people were in Hiroshima when the bomb went off. The explosion also destroyed many records. So, it's hard know how many people died. The US government estimated 70,000 deaths. The Japanese government estimated 140,000.

President Truman tells Americans about the bombing of Hiroshima on August 6, 1945.

Hiroshima lay in ruins. Sixteen hours later, President Truman spoke over the radio. He told Americans about the bombing. He told Japan's leaders to surrender. If they didn't, he said he would attack again. But Japan did not give up. So, US leaders planned to drop a second nuclear bomb.

The nuclear bomb dropped on August 9, 1945, weighed 10,000 pounds (4,500 kg).

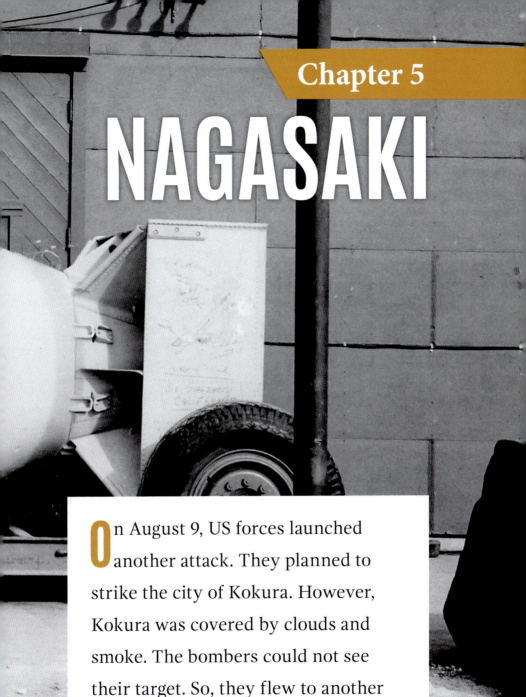

Chapter 5
NAGASAKI

On August 9, US forces launched another attack. They planned to strike the city of Kokura. However, Kokura was covered by clouds and smoke. The bombers could not see their target. So, they flew to another city instead.

The second bomb affected about 43 square miles (111 sq km) in and around Nagasaki.

The plane reached the city of Nagasaki. The sky was still cloudy. But then there was a break in the clouds. The plane dropped the bomb. It was off target. So, part of the city was spared. Even so, at least 40,000 people died instantly. Most were civilians.

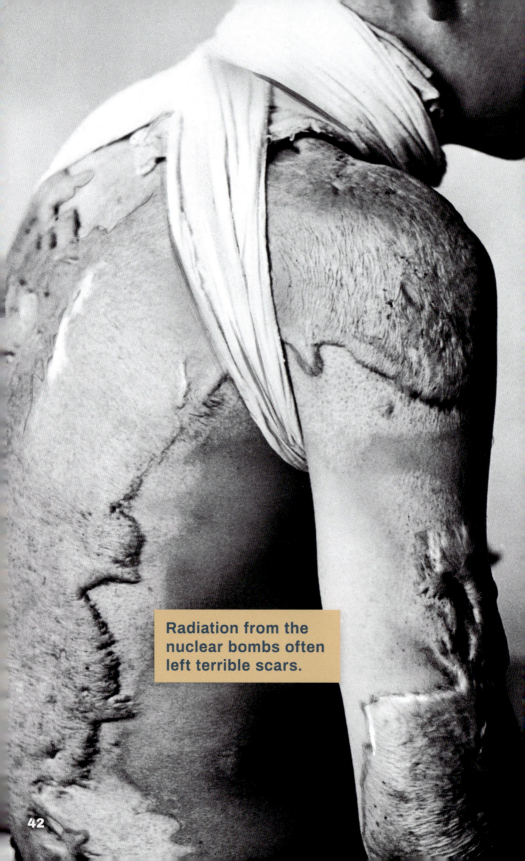

Radiation from the nuclear bombs often left terrible scars.

The US military made plans for more attacks. Scientists started building more nuclear bombs. But President Truman decided not to use them. He thought killing more civilians was too awful.

RADIATION SICKNESS

The two bombs killed at least 110,000 people instantly. Many more died in the months to come. Nuclear bombs release large amounts of radiation. This is a powerful form of energy. It makes people very ill. Another 100,000 people may have died from radiation sickness.

Japan's military leaders wanted to keep fighting. But Japan's emperor did not. He decided it was time to give up. On August 15, he announced Japan would stop fighting. A peace treaty was signed on September 2. The war was finally over.

MILITARY TAKEOVER

When the war ended, the US military took over Japan. US forces set up a new government for the country. Japan was not allowed to have a military. And it could not go to war. In 1952, the United States stepped back. It gave control of the country back to Japan. But the US military still has several bases in Japan.

US soldiers celebrate the end of World War II in August 1945.

Story Spotlight

DOUBLE SURVIVOR

On August 6, 1945, Tsutomu Yamaguchi was on a trip for work. He was in Hiroshima. The bomb exploded less than 2 miles (3.2 km) from him. Yamaguchi got burns on his chest. But he survived the blast. The next day, Yamaguchi went home. He lived in Nagasaki. On August 9, he survived the bombing there.

Yamaguchi later wrote books about his experience. He spoke out against nuclear bombs. Yamaguchi died in 2010. He was 93 years old.

Tsutomu Yamaguchi wrote poetry to deal with surviving the nuclear bombings.

Chapter 6
LEGACY

Dropping the bombs changed the world. In 1945, most Americans supported it. Today, many people still do. They say the bombings were awful. But they believe lives were saved. Many soldiers could have died in an invasion.

Countries have done more than 2,000 nuclear tests since 1945.

Other people do not agree. Some say Japan was ready to give up. Japan was surrounded. Its supplies were cut off.

Some people say racism played a role. They say US leaders wouldn't have used the bomb on a European country. But they felt okay using it against an Asian country.

Others think there should have been a public test. It could have shown the bomb's power without killing anyone.

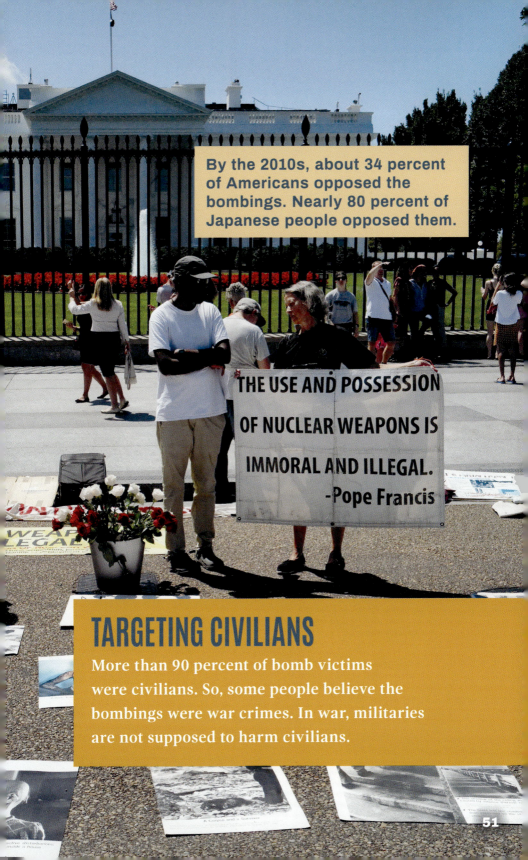

By the 2010s, about 34 percent of Americans opposed the bombings. Nearly 80 percent of Japanese people opposed them.

THE USE AND POSSESSION OF NUCLEAR WEAPONS IS IMMORAL AND ILLEGAL.
-Pope Francis

TARGETING CIVILIANS

More than 90 percent of bomb victims were civilians. So, some people believe the bombings were war crimes. In war, militaries are not supposed to harm civilians.

Nuclear bombs stayed important after the war. For example, the Soviet Union was a major power. It had been a US ally. But that changed by the late 1940s. The two nations became enemies. Both countries built many nuclear bombs. The bombs became more and more powerful.

TSAR BOMBA

In 1961, the Soviet Union tested a new bomb. It was called the Tsar Bomba. It was the biggest bomb in history. It was more than 3,000 times stronger than the bomb that hit Hiroshima.

The conflict between the United States and the Soviet Union was known as the Cold War.

Countries often tested nuclear bombs in the Pacific. They did lasting damage there.

In 1963, many countries signed a treaty. They agreed to ban most nuclear tests. Tests could still happen underground. But they could not happen on land. They could not happen underwater either.

STILL A THREAT

Nuclear bombs are still a threat today. There are more than 13,000 nuclear weapons in the world. Since 2006, North Korea has tested several bombs. In 2022, Russia invaded Ukraine. Russia's leader said he was ready for nuclear war.

The bombings remain an important part of Japan's history. Hiroshima has a memorial. It is a ruined building. After the bombing, it was the only building still standing in the area. Nagasaki has a memorial, too. There is a park and a museum. There is also a place to remember the dead.

People often visit these memorials. Like many people, they hope for peace. They hope for a world without nuclear weapons.

People attend a rally at Hiroshima's memorial in 2022 to oppose nuclear weapons.

TIMELINE

DECEMBER 1938 — Scientists discover it is possible to build a nuclear bomb.

DECEMBER 7, 1941 — Japan attacks Pearl Harbor. The United States enters World War II.

JANUARY 1942 — President Franklin D. Roosevelt approves the Manhattan Project.

JULY 16, 1945 — In New Mexico, Manhattan Project scientists test the world's first nuclear bomb.

AUGUST 6, 1945 — The United States drops a nuclear bomb on Hiroshima, Japan. Approximately 70,000 people die instantly. Many more die in the months to come.

AUGUST 9, 1945 — The United States drops a nuclear bomb on Nagasaki, Japan. Approximately 40,000 people die instantly. Many more die in the months to come.

AUGUST 15, 1945 — Japan's emperor announces that his country will surrender.

SEPTEMBER 2, 1945 — Japan signs a peace treaty, ending World War II.

COMPREHENSION QUESTIONS

Write your answers on a separate piece of paper.

1. Write a paragraph that explains the main ideas of Chapter 2.

2. Do you think the United States should have dropped nuclear bombs on Japan? Why or why not?

3. When was the first nuclear bomb tested?

    A. December 7, 1941
    B. July 16, 1945
    C. August 6, 1945

4. When did Harry Truman find out about the Manhattan Project?

    A. when he became vice president
    B. after President Roosevelt died
    C. after the bombing of Nagasaki

5. What does **conquered** mean in this book?

*Japan had already **conquered** several countries in Asia. Japan took over Korea in 1905. In 1931, Japan invaded China.*

    A. lost control of

    B. taken control of

    C. run away from

6. What does **surrender** mean in this book?

*He told Japan's leaders to **surrender**. If they didn't, he said he would attack again. But Japan did not give up.*

    A. to start fighting

    B. to keep fighting

    C. to give up

Answer key on page 64.

GLOSSARY

chain reaction
A series of events in which each action causes new actions.

civilians
People who are not part of the military.

emperor
A powerful ruler who controls a large area.

estimated
Made a guess when there was not enough information to figure out an exact number.

invaded
Entered a place using force.

leaflets
Pieces of paper with messages on them.

memorial
A structure built to remind people of a specific person or event.

peace deal
An agreement to end fighting. The agreement often explains what the winning side gains and what the losing side has to give up.

treaty
An agreement between two or more countries or groups.

war crimes
Serious crimes that happen during a war. These crimes include killing civilians and torturing prisoners.

TO LEARN MORE

BOOKS

Gaines, Ann Graham. *Harry S. Truman: Our 33rd President*. Mankato, MN: The Child's World, 2021.

London, Martha. *Atomic Bomb Survivor Stories*. Minneapolis: Abdo Publishing, 2022.

Roberts, Russell. *World War II in the Pacific*. Mendota Heights, MN: Focus Readers, 2023.

ONLINE RESOURCES

Visit **www.apexeditions.com** to find links and resources related to this title.

ABOUT THE AUTHOR

Nick Rebman is a writer and editor who lives in Minnesota.

INDEX

civilians, 15–16, 35, 41, 43, 51

firebombing, 16

Hiroshima, 4, 6, 9, 35, 37, 46, 52, 56

Kokura, 39

Manhattan Project, 21, 23–24, 28
memorial, 56

Nagasaki, 41, 46, 56
New Mexico, 24, 28
nuclear tests, 24, 28, 50, 52, 55

Okinawa, 19
Oppenheimer, J. Robert, 28

peace treaty, 44
Pearl Harbor, 10, 12

radiation, 43
Roosevelt, Franklin D., 20, 23

Soviet Union, 52

Truman, Harry S., 23, 26, 37, 43
Tsar Bomba, 52

war crimes, 15, 51

Yamaguchi, Tsutomu, 46

ANSWER KEY:
1. Answers will vary; 2. Answers will vary; 3. B; 4. B; 5. B; 6. C